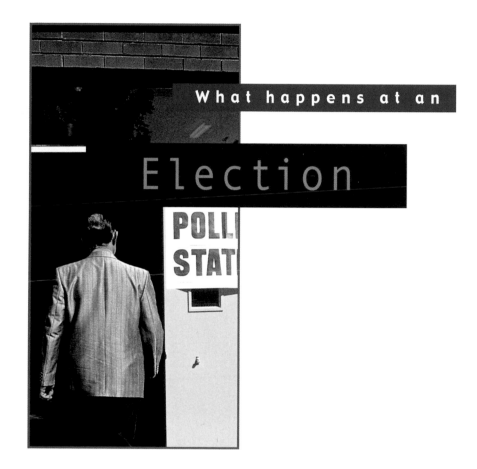

What happens at an

Election

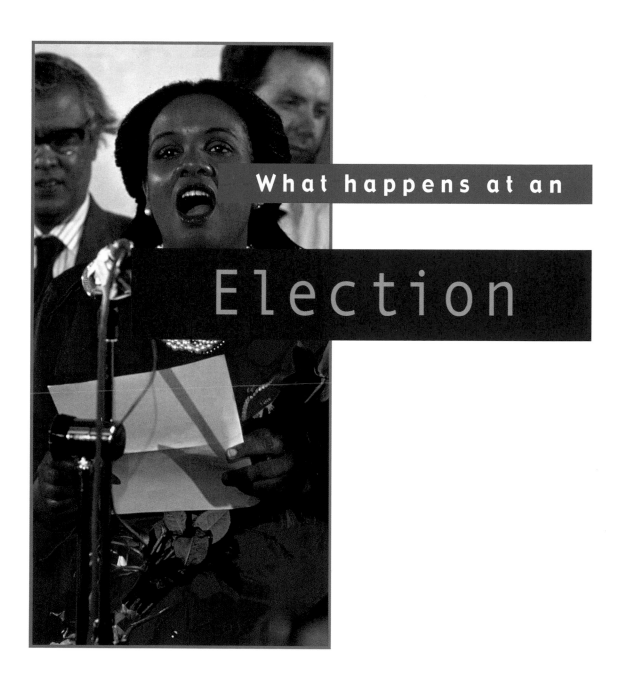

What happens at an

# Election

FRANKLIN WATTS
LONDON • SYDNEY

## About the author

Simon Adams lives in South London, where he served as a councillor on Lambeth Council for six years, and has voted in seven general elections and numerous local elections during his political life. He was educated at the London School of Economics and Bristol University, and is a full-time writer of children's non-fiction books.

## Key words

To help you find your way around this book, key words are printed in **bold**. You can find some of these words in the glossary on pages 30-31.

**Illustrations**  Alastair Taylor/The Inkshed

**Designer**  Magda Weldon
**Editor**  Penny Clarke
**Art Director**  Jonathan Hair
**Editor-in-Chief**  John C. Miles

© 2000 Franklin Watts

First published in 2000
by Franklin Watts
96 Leonard Street
London
EC2A 4XD

Franklin Watts Australia
14 Mars Road
Lane Cove
NSW 2066

ISBN 0 7496 3939 3

Dewey classification: 324

A CIP catalogue record
for this book is available
from the British Library.

Printed in Malaysia

# Contents

**The right to take part and vote in elections is one of the most important rights that people possess. Elections are at the heart of our democratic system of government, yet all too often we take them for granted.**

## The democratic process

A true **democracy** is a country in which everyone participates in **government**. That, however, would be impossible in a country with a population the size of Britain's, so instead of participating directly, we elect **representatives** to govern on our behalf.

In this way the government is both **chosen** by us and is **answerable** to us for what it does. If we do not like the government, we can **vote** it out of

PEOPLE AROUND THE WORLD watched in 1994 as black South Africans voted for the first time.

**office** at the next **election**. And the same is true for the Scottish Parliament, the Northern Irish, Welsh and London assemblies and of every local council. Without elections, there would be no democracy, and our government could do what it liked.

In Britain a **democratic system** seems the obvious way to run the government. But it is in fact a relatively recent invention: 200 years ago only two out of every 100 people had the vote, and it was not until 1918 that some women were allowed to vote. Full universal **adult suffrage** for everyone over 21 did not become law until 1928, and 18 year olds only got the vote in 1969.

## The importance of voting

Elsewhere in the world the **right to vote** is even more recent. Most people in Asia, Africa, the Caribbean and the Pacific could only vote when their countries received independence in the 1950s and 1960s.

In many Eastern European countries, people were only able to vote for the **candidates** and **political parties** of their choice after the collapse of communism in 1990. And in 1994, the world watched with admiration and awe as black South Africans stood patiently in line, some of them for the whole day, waiting to vote for the first time.

It is not just national politicians who are elected. **Members of the European Parliament** (MEPs) are elected from the European Union. **Local councillors** are elected to **county** and **district councils**, directors are elected to the boards of companies, trade unionists are elected to run their **union**, and school students are elected to **committees**.

This book looks at different types of elections and how you participate in them.

No one is sure when the first elections took place in Britain, but it is known that the Anglo-Saxons who invaded Britain in the 5th and 6th centuries often elected their leaders.

## Electing Parliament

The first recognisable **elections** in England took place in 1264, when two knights from each **shire** or county were summoned by the king to **Parliament**. In 1295 Edward I initiated the so-called **Model Parliament**, which contained two knights from each shire and two **citizens** from each borough or town.

The method of electing these representatives varied, but in 1429 the rules were standardised in each shire. It was agreed that everyone who owned land worth more than 40 shillings a year could vote, a rule that lasted until 1832. During this period, towns and cities received **royal charters** to run their own affairs, and held elections to their **councils**. In some towns the **councillors** elected **representatives to Parliament** themselves, while in others all those eligible to vote did so.

The main qualification for the **right to vote** in both parliamentary and local council elections was **property**. As women could not hold property, the rule meant in practice that only quite wealthy men were allowed to vote.

## A corrupt system

By the start of the 19th century the British **electoral system** was out of date. The large industrial towns

**The first recognisable elections in Britain took place in the thirteenth century.**

of the Midlands and north of England often had no councils and no **Members of Parliament (MPs)**, while some small towns had two MPs. Large landowners often picked the local MP, and elections were open to widespread **corruption**.

## Reform

The first steps to reform the system took place under the **Reform Act** of 1832. This extended the **franchise** (vote) to men from the middle classes and gave **representation** to larger industrial towns. Further Reform Acts were passed in 1867 and in 1884, although women were still not allowed to vote or stand for Parliament. **Secret ballots** were not introduced until 1872.

In 1918 the right to vote was extended: all men aged 21 and over and all women **ratepayers** or wives of ratepayers aged 30 and over gained the vote. Finally, in 1928 women achieved the same voting rights as men.

The age limit was lowered to 18 in 1969. It has been suggested by some people that it should be lowered to 16, when by law children become adults.

**A RIOTOUS ELECTION SCENE of the 1830s, from Charles Dickens' Sketches by Boz.**

Elections take place in Britain almost every day, but very few of them make the news. Some are purely local affairs, while others change governments and set the country on a different path altogether.

**Show of hands**

**Postal vote**

**Secret ballot**

**SOME TYPES OF ELECTION**

## Parliamentary elections

Every five years the **Prime Minister** must ask the **Queen** to dissolve the **House of Commons** and call a **general election**. The election can be called in less than five years if the Queen agrees.

All MPs stand down and fight an election in their **constituency** (the area of the country that they represent in **Parliament**) in order to become an MP again. The number of **seats** in the House of Commons varies slightly; in 1997 it was 659.

General elections are the most important elections held in Britain, as the government of the country can change if the **party** previously in **opposition** manages to win a **majority** of **seats**.

**By-elections** are held in a single constituency if the MP of the constituency dies, resigns or retires before a general election.

At a **regional** level, elections are held for the Scottish Parliament and the Welsh, Northern Irish and London **assemblies** once every four years.

**Local government** elections for county, district and borough **councils** are held either annually – with one-third of the **councillors** up for election each year – or every three or four years, depending on the type of council.

## Political parties and trade unions

Apart from elections for various types of government, elections occur in a vast range of different organisations. Members of **political parties** elect their leaders and some other senior officers, such as **treasurers** or **chairs**, often at their **annual conference** held in a seaside resort.

**Trade union** members elect their **general secretaries** and members of their **executive (ruling) committees**, again often at their annual or biennial conferences. Members of major industrial and commercial organisations, such as the **Trades Union Congress (TUC)**, the regional branches of the **Confederation of British Industry (CBI)**, and the **British Chamber of Commerce** all elect their leaders. So too do members of many trade and employers' associations.

## Other elections

Members of some large national organisations, such as the **National Trust**, have the right to vote for the executive committee. At a local level members elect the **management committee** of a sports or social club or a voluntary or charitable organisation. Finally, if you own shares in a company or have an account with a building society, you can elect the **directors** of the management boards.

In other words, join any organisation – local or national – and at some point or other you will be asked to vote in an election.

**Elections aren't just about government – many clubs and voluntary organisations elect their management boards.**

**Voting is not just a simple matter of turning up on the day to cast a vote in a polling station. There are many different ways of voting, and lots of rules that spell out who can and cannot vote.**

## Different systems

Most elections in Britain are conducted under the **first past the post system**. Every **elector** has one vote and the **candidate** who gains the most votes wins the election, even if a **majority** of the electorate voted for other candidates. Some people think that this winner-takes-all system is unfair.

Another system of voting is **proportional representation (PR)**. PR tries to achieve a balance between the total votes cast for a **political party** and the number of its candidates that are elected, often by grouping **constituencies** together so that they return more than one representative.

In elections to the **Scottish Parliament,** for example, electors vote twice: once for a candidate in a single constituency and once for a party in a wider region.

## Who can vote?

Any UK **citizen** registered to vote in the **constituency** or **ward** where an election is taking place and who is 18 or over can vote in a **local, parliamentary** or **European Union (EU)** election.

Irish and Commonwealth citizens resident in the UK can vote in every election. UK citizens resident abroad can vote in parliamentary and EU elections.

**Unlike some countries, such as Australia and Belgium, voting in the UK is not compulsory.**

**FIRST PAST THE POST can be unfair. The winning candidate is the one with the most votes. Electors who voted for other candidates (glum faces) can outnumber those who voted for the winner (smiling faces).**

## Who cannot vote

Members of the House of Lords cannot vote in parliamentary elections, although they can vote in local, regional and European elections. Prisoners, patients detained under mental health legislation and people convicted within the previous five years of illegal election practices cannot vote.

## The electoral register

In order to vote, your name must be on the **electoral register** or **roll**. This is compiled by the **election officer** in your local **town hall**, who sends out **registration forms** to every household in the early autumn. These must be filled in with the name of every resident who is or will become 18 in the year the register is in force.

If you are away during an election or are unable to vote in person, you can apply for a **postal vote** or nominate a **proxy** (substitute) to vote for you.

Every local, parliamentary or European parliamentary election in Britain takes place on a Thursday. On that day, electors go to the polling station to cast their votes, but where do they go and how does it work?

## What are polling stations?

**Polling stations** are ordinary buildings adapted for the day. **Local councils** run elections, so they often use their own buildings, such as the **town hall**, **schools**, **libraries** and similar venues. **Church halls** and scout huts are also used, as are **day centres**.

In rural areas, where there are few suitable buildings, mobile libraries and post buses are used. Occasionally, privately owned buildings, such as offices or farm buildings, are hired for the day.

## A good polling station ?

A polling station has to be visible from the street, well known in the local neighbourhood, and accessible to those with a physical disability or who find it difficult to walk.

However, many polling stations were built before access became important, so they often have steps up to the door or an entrance too narrow for a wheelchair. In most cases, therefore, people with a disability cannot get into a polling station unaided.

A polling station also has to be local, because if people have to walk a long way to vote, they might not bother. Each polling station usually serves between 1,500–2,000 voters.

**A POLLING STATION always includes booths for marking ballot papers and sealed boxes to deposit them in.**

**For some Parliamentary by-elections, voter turnout has been as low as only 20 per cent.**

ON ELECTION DAY, local polling stations are clearly marked so that everyone knows where to vote.

## Reforming the system

In recent years, the total number of people **turning out to vote** has declined steadily from 83.9 per cent in the **general election** of 1950 to 71.5 per cent in 1997. For **local government elections** the figure is rarely more than 40 per cent.

The government is therefore investigating placing polling stations where they are more accessible and visible, such as in railway stations or supermarkets, so that more people might be encouraged to vote.

They are considering allowing voting at weekends and staggering voting over different days so that people can vote when it suits them. Another idea is to get rid of the fixed electoral roll, which requires an elector to be resident in a place on 10 October in the year before the election, and replace it with a system that allows people to register at any time.

## Including everyone

**Internet** and **telephone voting** are also under consideration, as are plans to make it easier to **vote by post**. The homeless and other excluded groups, such as travellers, will also get the right to vote, while more help will be given to people with various disabilities, to partially sighted people and to those who cannot read or write.

These and other ideas should make it easier for people to vote in a place that is convenient, local and, above all, accessible. It is hoped that, as a result, the number of people voting might rise.

Getting ready for an election involves a huge amount of work by many different people: officials, political parties, candidates, agents and others. So who does what, and when?

## An election is called

The date of a **general election** is chosen by the **Prime Minister**; the date for a **by-election** is decided by party managers in the **House of Commons**. **Local council elections** are always held on the first Thursday of May; **council by-elections** take place on a Thursday decided by the **electoral officer.**

The electoral officer at the town hall publicises the timetable, stating when **nominations** for **candidates** must be in. She or he also names the polling stations, organises **ballot boxes** and the printing of the **ballot papers** and checks the electoral register.

**BALLOT PAPERS** have the name of each election candidate printed on them, plus a space for the voter to mark an 'X' for their choice.

The electoral officer also arranges the printing of **polling cards** which are posted to every **elector**. These tell electors their **polling number**, the date and time of the election, what the election is for and where the polling station is. Although you can vote without the card, it helps the polling officer find your name on the electoral register and tick it off, thus ensuring that no one votes pretending to be you.

Once your nomination is accepted, you are a candidate for election and will have no time to play or rest until the election is over.

## The parties prepare

Meanwhile **political parties** arrange the **selection** of their candidates. Some candidates stand as **independents**, but most stand for a party, which means that most parliamentary and council elections are contested by Labour, Conservative or Liberal Democrat candidates. There are the Scottish Nationalists in Scotland, Plaid Cymru in Wales and a range of Unionist, Nationalist and Republican parties in Northern Ireland.

Parliamentary elections also attract a range of **fringe** parties, standing on issues as varied as anti-European Union to the benefits of yogic flying. Far right and far left parties also field candidates, as does the environmental Green Party.

A candidate has to be **nominated** by ten electors in the ward or constituency for which she or he is standing. These electors fill in and sign the **nomination form**. A candidate can also appoint an **election agent** to handle all the official paperwork.

## Who can stand?

Anyone can **stand** for election provided they are 21 or over and are on the electoral register. Anyone standing for a council must live or work in the area served by the council. Candidates in parliamentary elections can live anywhere in the UK.

You cannot stand for election to a council if you work for that council, for the civil service or hold a highly paid job with another local authority. You cannot stand as an MP if you are bankrupt, in prison for more than one year, a member of the House of Lords, a clergyman in the Anglican or Roman Catholic churches, a police officer, a member of the armed services, a civil servant or a judge.

**Candidates for election have to persuade the electors in their constituencies or wards that they are the right person for the job and that they and their party have the right policies.**

**The most important task for a candidate is to meet the voters.**

## The manifesto

Each **political party** produces a **manifesto**, which spells out what it stands for and what it would do if it won the election. This manifesto can be a few paragraphs or many pages in length, and is usually written in very general terms. Political parties rarely make definite promises in case they fail to deliver them when in office.

To make that national manifesto more personal, individual candidates often issue their own manifesto, stating what they would do in the constituency or ward. A candidate's manifesto often includes personal details about their life and background, and why they would make a good Member of Parliament or councillor if elected.

## Publicity

Election campaigns are often fought in a blizzard of paper. Party workers print colour **posters**, produce rolls of **stickers**, buy and wear **rosettes** in party colours and publish a variety of **leaflets**.

Increasingly, because computers make it so easy, candidates use **mailshots** to target specific groups of voters. For example, a candidate may write a letter to all the residents of a street. The idea is that more people will read a letter than a leaflet.

**THE TRADITIONAL WAY of campaigning – a lively doorstep debate between candidate and voter.**

## Meeting the electorate

A successful campaign is one where the candidate talks to as many people as possible and becomes so well known that people feel enthusiastic enough to vote for him or her. The traditional way of doing this was to knock on doors and talk to people face to face. Nowadays, candidates and their supporters also use the phone to contact people, organise street stalls or stage high-profile **walkabouts** in order to attract attention. They also publicly **debate** issues with their **opponents** and try to attend as many local meetings as they can.

## Modern campaigning

Until quite recently, campaigns were high-profile events that people cared about and scrutinised closely. Today people care less about politics than they used to. As a result, candidates have to work harder to attract people's attention, and have to make their message short so that it is not lost or ignored among all the other distractions.

In a general election campaign most electors will never meet any of the candidates. So how do people know who the candidates are? How much money can be spent trying to persuade them who to vote for?

## Why people vote

At the start of any **election campaign** at least half the electors have already made up their minds. They might be **members** of a political party, or always support a particular party, so they need no persuading to vote for it again.

Up to one-quarter of the electorate never vote at all, leaving a final quarter who have to make up their minds. They read newspapers and watch the news on television, but need to be persuaded that one party is better than another. Often it is one particular **issue** that persuades them who to vote for. It is these voters – known as **swing voters** – who decide the outcome of an election. If they do not swing in favour of your candidate, she or he will not win.

## How much can be spent?

The law concerning how much a candidate can spend in an election is complex. In order to stand for Parliament, for example, a candidate must pay a **deposit** of £500, which is forfeited if she or he does not get at least 5 per cent of the vote. Each candidate can spend up to £4,965, plus 4.2p for each urban elector, or 5.6p for each rural elector, making a total of about £8,500 for each constituency.

**In the 1997 general election, the two main political parties together spent £30 million on television and press advertising alone.**

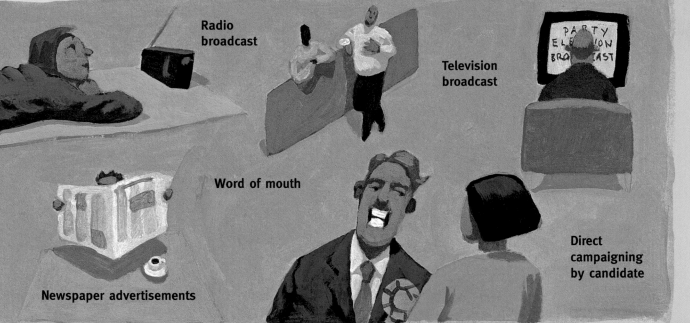

Radio broadcast

Television broadcast

Word of mouth

Direct campaigning by candidate

Newspaper advertisements

**THERE ARE MANY WAYS of influencing public opinion in an election.**

However, there is currently no limit on the amount a political party can spend on television or billboard advertising or on national **campaigning** – rich parties can spend as much as they can earn or fundraise without breaking any rules.

## Changing the system

Proposals currently before the House of Commons aim to remove this anomaly by limiting **overall spending**. A party **contesting** every UK constituency will be limited to £19.77 million, which is £30,000 for each of the 659 seats. This change will reduce the ability of a rich political party to 'buy' a general election.

At the end of an election, every candidate has to hand in detailed **accounts** showing how much was spent on such items as postage, hire of rooms, printing and phone bills.

If any candidates spend more than the **limit**, or are accused of falsifying their accounts, they risk being taken to court and losing their seats if they were successful.

The people who work hardest on election day are the people who organise and staff the polling stations. Their work is crucial in making sure that everything runs smoothly.

**ONCE IN THE POLLING STATION, people go to the polling booths and mark their ballot papers.**

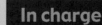

## In charge

The person in charge of running an election is the **electoral officer** at the local **town hall**. She or he runs a large team of staff who help out on the day. Each polling station has its own **presiding officer**, who makes sure everything goes smoothly.

Before the polling station opens at 7.00am for a general election and 8.00am for a council election, the presiding officer must ensure that it is ready.

> **Election officers can mark a ballot paper on an elector's behalf if they cannot do it for themselves.**

The **polling booths** must be put up; each one must have pencils with which people can mark their **ballot papers**, the sealed **ballot boxes** must be put out and large notices must be put up outside the polling station to tell people where to vote. Most importantly of all, the presiding officer must get the **electoral register** and ballot papers ready.

## How to vote

When people come into the polling station they hand their **polling card** to the **returning officer** seated at the table. If they do not have their card, they give their name and address. The officer finds their name on the electoral register, ticks it off and stamps the ballot paper with a mark to make sure that fraudulent ballot papers are not smuggled in.

The elector then takes the ballot paper and goes over to the polling booth. Here he or she marks the paper in secret and then puts it into the ballot box, which is on a table next to the returning officer.

On some election days two or more elections may be held at the same time: in this case, the ballot papers are different colours to distinguish them, although they are all put into the same ballot box.

## Help for those who need it

Election officers help people in and out of the polling station if they have a mobility problem. If the elector cannot get into the polling station, the officer can bring the ballot paper and box outside.

When the **poll** closes at 10.00pm for general elections and 9.00pm for council elections, the presiding officer at each polling station has one vital job left: to get the ballot box to the town hall or building where the **count** is to take place.

After all the excitement and activity of an election campaign, election day itself is something of an anticlimax for the candidates. But they cannot afford to relax – there is still much to be done.

## The candidate's role

The first thing for the **candidate** to do is vote. It is surprising how often candidates have to be reminded that they too are electors and can vote for themselves! Once that is done, the candidate's role is to be seen about the **constituency**, distinguished by a large **rosette** in party colours. Some candidates try to visit all the **polling stations**, others drive round in a car with a megaphone on the roof, encouraging people to go and vote.

## The party workers

While the candidate is out and about on his or her rounds, **party workers** are busy. Well-organised political parties have a **campaign room** in each constituency and ward where they motivate workers and supporters.

First thing in the morning, before the polls open, every house is **leafleted** with a 'Don't forget to vote' leaflet with the name and party of the candidate in large type. Volunteers then take turns to sit outside every polling station throughout the day to write down the **polling numbers** of those who vote (voters can refuse to give their numbers).

These numbers are then collected by a party worker, often on a bike or motorbike, and rushed

**Once the campaigning and debating is over, candidates wait for voters to make up their minds.**

back to the campaign room, where they are checked against lists of known supporters. Later on in the day, party workers visit those electors who have not voted – the practice is known as **knocking-up** – to make sure they get out to vote, offering them a lift to and from the polling station in a car as an incentive. Using polling numbers, parties can usually work out roughly how their candidate is doing and what the result is likely to be.

As the day goes on, more and more supporters turn up to help. In the last few hours, they chase up those who have still not voted, and make every effort to get every last voter out. By the time the polls close they are all exhausted, waiting nervously for the **count** and the **final result**.

**ON ELECTION DAY, each candidate works hard to try and convince everyone to vote for them. Here are some of the ways.**

Telling people to go and vote

Knocking-up

Last-minute campaigning

Loudspeaker vans roaming the streets to get the message across

After the polls close, the election reaches its climax as votes are counted and a result is declared. This is the time when history is made, as winners claim their prizes while losers retire to lick their wounds.

## The count

As soon as the **polling stations** close, the **ballot boxes** are rushed to the **count** by car or taxi. Most counts take place the same evening, but some happen on the following day.

At a general election, some constituencies rush for the honour to be the first to declare a **result**; the usual winner is a small inner-city constituency like Sunderland South. The count itself takes place in a town hall, large civic building or even a huge exhibition centre, such as the NEC in Birmingham.

**TELLERS are usually council or bank workers used to counting precisely and efficiently.**

> **Counting officers will accept any mark on a ballot paper – even a smiley face – if the voter's intention is clear.**

When the **ballot boxes** arrive, they are unsealed and opened. The **tellers** – as the counting staff are known – count the number of **ballot papers** in the box against the number issued at the polling station. When it is confirmed that the numbers match, the tellers begin to sort the papers out, placing them in piles for each candidate. These are then counted into bundles and wrapped.

The bundles are then placed in pairs in a long tray. At this stage, as the trays fill up, it is possible to see roughly which party is winning.

## The result

When the **count** has been completed, the **candidates** and their **agents** are called together and given the **result**. If the final result is very close, the second-placed candidate can ask for a **recount** in the hope that a mistake has been made.

The **returning officer** for each constituency is the mayor for a parliamentary election or the chief executive of the council for a council election. Often, however, the result is announced by the council's **election officer**, acting as the **deputy returning officer**. She or he states the name of the constituency or ward and then reads out the names of each candidate in alphabetical order and the number of votes.

It is customary for the **winning candidate** to make a short speech, thanking the returning officer and all the counting staff, the police for security and, of course, the voters for their support. Most election speeches are short and non-contentious.

When the speeches are over, the celebrations and commiserations begin as the winning candidate begins a new life as a Member of Parliament or a councillor.

**Elections are held throughout the world, but different countries use different systems. Some countries use the first past the post system, while others use various forms of proportional representation.**

Two very different electoral systems are those used in France and the USA.

## France – two-stage voting

In France, elections for the French parliament and president take place on successive Sundays. On the first Sunday voters chose from a long list of candidates. After the votes are counted, a winner is declared if she or he has more than 50 per cent of the total vote. If no one achieves this, the two candidates who won the most votes go forward to a second ballot.

This allows political parties to do deals to support each other in particular seats and presents an elector with a clear choice between two candidates, often from either side of the political divide.

## The USA – the electoral college

Electors in the United States do not elect their president directly but through an electoral college. Every four years, on the first Tuesday of November, electors throughout the country vote for their presidential candidate. Their votes are counted up in each state and a state winner is declared.

Then a number of electors for each state equal to its total representation in Congress (two senators plus up to 50 or more members of the House of Representatives) cast their votes for that candidate on 6 January the following year.

USA

Electoral college

FRANCE

Two-stage
voting

DIMANCHE
**19**
JANVIER

DIMANCHE
**26**
JANVIER

AUSTRALIA

Compulsory voting

**THERE ARE MANY SYSTEMS of
election in use around the world.**

This indirect system produces some odd results. Many recent presidents, including John Kennedy in 1960, Richard Nixon in 1968 and Bill Clinton in both 1992 and 1996 have won majorities in the electoral college but did not have a majority of the total vote.

## Compulsory voting

In Britain an elector can choose whether or not to vote. In a number of countries, including Australia, Austria, Belgium, Brazil and Greece, voting is compulsory in some or all elections.

In Australia, it is an offence not to vote in federal elections (that is, elections to the Australian national parliament). Anyone who is unable to provide a 'valid and sufficient reason' why they have not voted is fined $20 (about £8) by the election's returning officer, or $50 (£20) plus costs if the case is taken to the Magistrates' court.

Supporters of compulsory voting argue that voting is a civic duty and should therefore be mandatory. Others argue that it is undemocratic to force people to vote.

# Glossary

**ballot box**　The black metal box into which completed ballot papers are put. The box is sealed before the election starts and is only opened at the official count.

**ballot paper**　The official voting paper used to record a person's vote. On the paper are the names of all the candidates and a space for the elector to place an 'X' against one of them.

**by-election**　Election called to fill a vacancy in Parliament or a local council, for example when the post-holder dies or resigns.

**candidate**　Someone who stands for election.

**canvass**　To seek a person's vote and support in an election.

**committee**　Group of people elected to do a particular job, such as running an organisation.

**constituency**　The geographical area represented by a Member of Parliament (MP). Electors here are known as constituents.

**councillor**　Elected member of the local council who represents a ward; also known as a member.

**democracy**　Government by the people or their elected representatives.

**deposit**　In a general election each candidate must pay a deposit of £500 in order to stand. This deposit is returned to them if they win 5 per cent or more of the total vote, but they lose the money if they fall below this figure.

**election**　The selection by vote of a person to represent people in Parliament, local council or another organisation.

**elector** Person on the electoral register or list of members who is able to vote in an election.

**electoral register** The official list of all those eligible to vote. The register is arranged street by street in alphabetical and numerical order.

**general election** Election held when Parliament is dissolved and every MP has to face re-election. In Britain general elections must be held every five years.

**knocking-up** The practice on election day of party workers knocking on supporters' doors to make sure they go to vote.

**local council** Group of councillors elected to govern a city, town, rural district or county in Britain.

**manifesto** Public statement of aims, policies and objectives issued by political parties and candidates in advance of an election.

**MP** Member of Parliament elected to represent a constituency in the House of Commons.

**polling booth** Wooden table on which electors mark their ballot papers. It is shielded on three sides to protect the elector's privacy.

**polling station** Building used to hold an election on polling day. Each polling station is used by the electors of one polling district in a ward.

**proportional representation** System of voting that tries to balance the total votes cast for a political party with the total number of candidates that are elected.

**seat** The parliamentary constituency held by an MP is known as a seat because an MP sits in the House of Commons.

**teller** Person who counts ballot papers after the polls have closed in an election.

**ward** An area that elects local councillors to represent them.

## ACKNOWLEDGMENTS
The author wishes to acknowledge the help and advice given by Len Lewis, Electoral Services Manager of the London Borough of Lambeth, in the preparation of this book.